IMPRESSIONS OF SALZBURG

Impressions of
SALZBURG

INTRODUCTORY ESSAY BY ALFRED KOMAREK
PHOTOGRAPHS BY HERBERT PIRKER

PINGUIN-VERLAG, INNSBRUCK

CONTENTS

SPIRITUALITY AND SENSUOUSNESS

Other cities are surrounded by mountains, Salzburg envelops its own: the Mönchsberg, the Festungsberg, the Nonnberg, the Rainberg and the Kapuzinerberg. Rocky precipices and high ridges fit into the picture, as though on the third day of Creation it was already quite clear where the built-up townscape would require natural heightening in the distant future. Since time immemorial Salzburg has subjected the earth in a manner as reverent as it is majestic. Those prince archbishops who, as lords spiritual and temporal, built the city according to their own ideas, destroying and renewing, were self-assured enough to alter mountains, too.

Above the Neutor gateway to the old city, opening the way through the Mönchsberg, vertical incisions can still be discerned in the rock. In the 17th century Max Gandolf von Kuenburg was pleased by the idea of having the Mönchsberg sawn into two parts in order to separate it, equipped with its own fortifications, from Hohensalzburg. A throng of moderately motivated beggars and soldiers went to work so listlessly, however, that the startling project soon came to an inconspicuous end. But one hundred years later Archbishop Siegmund Graf Schrattenbach really could no longer see why he should make a detour between the Residenz and his villa in the Riedenburg instead of having his coach driven through the mountain. After a good eight months of construction work the tunnel breakthrough succeeded, proud portals were added and above the portrait of the archbishop runs the wording: "Te saxa loquuntur" – the stones speak of you.

Salzburg would be nothing without the power of its princes of the Church. The citizens of the town were for centuries replete, affluent, self-assured and rebellious, but they had to cower before their pious lords. When there was conflict, the archbishop retired menacingly to the fortress. Leonhard von Keutschach, for instance, he whose insignia was a leafy turnip, courteously invited the city councillors and mayor – all dreaming of a free imperial city – to dine at court. Then he shouted them down and had them bound to sledges and taken to Radstadt in the biting cold of winter. Narrowly having escaped beheading, the citizens were readily willing to think of privileges no longer.

Wolf Dietrich tackled the realization of his princely city with a lack of consideration that was as brilliant as it was destructive. More than fifty town houses were demolished to make room for squares and when the archbishop was brought the alarming news that the Romanesque cathedral was burning, he remarked casually, "If it is burning, then let it burn." He had the human remains from the old cathedral cemetery tipped into the Salzach and only reluctantly did he make an exception for venerable relics: they lay in heaps in an outer room of the Residenz. When the last prince archbishop, Hieronymus Colloredo, had to cede Salzburg to the French, he providently had twenty-five barrels made to transport his money, modestly proved content with porcelain, the silver plate already having been taken to safety, and finally departed in touching simplicity, accompanied by only one valet. But Salzburg, that work of art pleasing to God, kept its radiance even in times of provincial insignificance and today no one doubts that the city has the unyielding whims of mighty lords to thank for its beauty, a loveliness which even the most ferocious constructional sins cannot destroy and which remains unaffected by kitsch or commerce. That blend of feudal self-realization and noble spirituality, playful earnestness and earnest play is omnipre-

sent. This very special atmosphere also fascinated those princes who kissed the stirring beauty Salzburg fully awake in 1920, tenderly at first, then ardently and passionately: Hugo von Hofmannsthal, Richard Strauss, Hermann Bahr and Max Reinhardt are numbered among the founders of the Salzburg Festival. It began as an austerely contemplative undertaking and today embraces and pervades its home so comprehensively that some can hardly restrain themselves for elitist enthusiasm and others find their breath taken away by so much cultural ballyhoo. When Death first reached for Everyman in the Domplatz, it was a charity performance and the actors received a souvenir instead of a fee, Werner Krauss gladly accepting lederhosen. The young festival's artistic fire endured harsh financial straits and, unimpressed, the love of drama did not even halt before the private lives of the artists. Max Reinhardt moved into the somewhat dilapidated Schloß Leopoldskron, renovating and furnishing it to the best of his ability and, rather than simply living here, he truly resided. His nightly festivities gathered together Austria's most glittering stage personalities, blending artistic performances and the profound delights of the palate in baroque opulence and combining sparkling society life with intelligent discussion. Egon Friedell once eyed with astonishment this dream of flickering candlelight, lackeys and innumerable white swans on the dark water and acknowledged, "I knew Max Reinhardt when he was still living in rented rooms, with only one change of suit and at the most two or three swans."
The festival developed like other artistic institutions in the land: actors' fees rose and the price of tickets vied with subsidy requirements. In 1925 Clemens Holzmeister built the first Festspielhaus and in 1960 the new building was opened: concrete and rock fused in architectonic unity. The growth limits have not been reached yet; there are still a couple of dates free for further festivals, major

and minor; not yet is every palace, every square, every park a stage. No one should be reproached for this culturally touristic deluge, however, not the artists who succumb to the charms of this irresistibly theatrical city, nor the benefactors and organizers who bring fame and currency to the place and certainly not the guests who come not in order to get on Salzburg people's nerves, but who invest heartily in order to treat themselves to a special experience. At any rate Salzburg cannot be slain, the enchantment remains: blithe, southern gaiety, its light radiating from the facades, and the poised, private elegance of the old city.

There is a noble, firmly established order in everything and anyone surveying rooftops, domes and spires from the fortress soon finds his way. The Domplatz, Kapitelplatz, Residenzplatz and Mozartplatz form the princely city. The monastic city pushes towards the rock with the Franciscan monastery and St. Peter's, followed on the left by the festival precinct with the old University district in front. Following the Getreidegasse, the burghers' city nestles around the other parts of the town and continues on the right bank of the Salzach. The view northwards from the back of the fortress falls on the Nonntal area and on friendly meadows with Schloß Leopoldskron. Behind the stylish building of the municipal pensioners' home the narrow blue ribbon of the Almkanal can be divined. This amazing feat of hydraulic engineering was laid out for Salzburg's water supply in the mid-12th century and has operated ever since without interruption. A tunnel conducts the cool water through the Mönchsberg, it comes into daylight by the old mill of St. Peter's and it supplies the horse pond on the Kapitelplatz. Until the 19th century the Almkanal also served the refuse disposal: once a week water was conducted through the alleyways and washed the accumulated dirt into the Salzach. Back to the fortress of Hohensalzburg, however.

It has long cast off its threatening features and is content to crown the city's silhouette with stony dignity, answering the carillon deep down below with a melodious bellow. The "Salzburger Stier" is responsible for this; Austria's oldest remaining open-air organ, its revered chords originally signalized the opening and closing of the fortress gates. The history of Hohensalzburg fortress, 542 metres above the city, started with a wooden structure in the 11th century. Only a few decades later stonework strengthened the site which was rebuilt and enlarged again and again in the following six hundred years. Leonhard von Keutschach was the most active of the prince archbishops to command the castle. He fortified the ring walls with powerful towers, added new gates and had a deep moat hewn out of the rock. Two chapels lent the proper piety to this bellicosity. His Grace also ensured that the interior of the fortress relinquished its severity, becoming almost comfortable. The quarrelsome ruler knew what he was doing: frequently enough the pent-up anger of his many enemies made it seem advisable to reside behind impenetrable walls above their furious heads. More than a hundred years later Wolf Dietrich von Raichenau was a person of a very different nature who formed the city's countenance afresh, but showed very little interest in the fortress. He did well in this, having to experience the walls from the inside as a prisoner for five agonizingly long years at the end of his life. Without the fortress Salzburg would be a disappointingly harmless city. Its name was, however, acquired from the long vanished walls of the "Salzachburg" which stood on the Nonnberg in the days of the *Völkerwanderung*, the name "Salzburg" thus deriving.

The ancient abbey of St. Peter's, close by the rock face of the Mönchsberg, also helped to write the beginning of Salzburg's history. Even in the Roman Juvavum there were Christians in the area of the old city of Salzburg. On his travels in 407 Saint Severin found monks and a monastery here. No one knows exactly when Rupertus came from Worms to receive the area as a gift from Duke Theodo of Bavaria; it might have been at the beginning of the 7th century. At any rate, he was the first abbot of St. Peter's whom we know of and he was also Bishop of Salzburg.

The most famous of his successors was an Irishman – Virgil, builder of the first cathedral in Salzburg. He bore the nickname, highly suspicious in conservative circles, "Feiergil the geometer" and he did all honour to his reputation by claiming that there were antipodes. Even such a man of scientific bent could not imagine a round planet, but why should a disc-shaped earth not have life at both sides? This came to the ears of Virgil's arch enemy, Boniface, primate of Germany, and he reported it gleefully to the Pope who promptly threatened to excommunicate Virgil and to forbid him to exercise the office of priest. It did not come to that, but henceforth the bishop's see was no longer occupied by Irish Scots, but by Anglo-Saxon-Frankish Benedictines. In subsequent centuries St. Peter's became a centre of learning. The industrious school of calligraphy created the requirements for a library of note and even the tradition – founded by Virgil – of peering beyond the confines of Catholic doctrine remained alive: one of the abbots, Johann von Staupnitz, was Martin Luther's superior in Erfurt and Wittenberg and remained on friendly terms with him in Salzburg.

At the beginning of the 17th century Benedictines from St. Peter's played a major part in establishing the old Salzburg University which existed until 1810. Today, the Collegium Benedictinum is a significant seat of learning for brothers in the faith from the German-speaking area.

In view of all this dry erudition, it is not really surprising that the St. Peter's "Stiftskeller" probably constitutes

Europe's oldest surviving inn: it was first mentioned in documents of 803.

Far from prompting painful sadness, the little cemetery of St. Peter's is one of those burial sites which impart a feeling of a gentle refuge – in life as in death. Even memories of Mozart sound without bitterness through the stillness. The Haffner family of merchants have their last resting place here; it was for them that the "Haffner Serenade" was created. Another tomb bears the name Hagenauer and it was in that family's house in the Getreidegasse that the composer was born. Mozart's sister, Nannerl, is buried in the communal vault and Michael Haydn also rests here. The walls of the Chapel of St. Margaret bear gravestones with famous Salzburg names: Keutschach, Kuenburg, Alt. Window openings are visible in the cliff face that forms the edge of the cemetery and a little wooden turret presses against the rugged rock. The catacombs tell of the first Christians in Salzburg. The secret sites of their devotions, the Chapel of St. Gertraud with its earnest, venerable stone seats and the Maximus Chapel higher up – a martyr's grave served as altar here – were entirely hidden by the mountain until a fall of rock exposed them.

Persecution, violence, daring hiding places – Salzburg's history is not that of a complacently pious provincial town. Here, in the field of tension between north and south, on a significant trading route, with the riches of salt in the nearby Dürrnberg, with gold and silver treasures in the Tauern valleys, there was never room for secluded contemplation. Even in the early days of settlement, the Neolithic, Salzburg proved to be an attractive stage for appearances by various cultural groups: Danubian culture and Bandkeramik, corded ware, Mondsee culture, bell beaker culture and others. Even then the occurrence of salt was important, later precious metals, too, and, with the Illyrians, iron. Thanks to "white gold" the Celts lived in the lap of luxury, developing a superior culture and cultivating international trading contacts. Strengthened again after Celtic conquests, Rome reacted to this development with increasing covetousness. With the capture of the kingdom of Noricum the area became Roman, the Celtic settlement on the Rainberg declined and in 15 B.C. there grew up on the banks of the Salzach that Juvavum with which the history of the city of Salzburg begins in the strict sense. The turmoils of the *Völkerwanderung* brought Juvavum to ruins. When Rupert founded St. Peter and Salzburg flourished as a new bishopric, a blend of temporal and spiritual power emerged in the field of tension between Emperor and Pope and this was to define Salzburg for centuries. In 996 Archbishop Hartwig secured marketing and minting rights for the town and in the early 13th century Archbishop Eberhard II accumulated property so energetically that he created the basis for an independent principality in the hands of the bishops. From then on Salzburg became a changing reflection of the visions and moods of its spiritual lords, influenced but marginally by the citizens who were by no means powerless, but who did well to look up respectfully to the fortress.

In that line of eighty-seven archbishops who followed Saint Rupert to the present day many famous names have accompanied us down through history. Leonhard von Keutschach, the security-conscious renewer of the fortress, Wolf Dietrich von Raichenau, the town planner obsessed with building, and Markus Sittikus of Hohenems, a truly baroque personality, associated with the reconstruction of the cathedral no less than with the erection of the palace of Hellbrunn. With an iron hand Paris Lodron preserved Salzburg from the terrors of the Thirty Years War, Johann Ernst Count Thun employed the services of that famous architect, Johann Bernhard Fischer von Erlach, and Franz Anton Prince Harrach summoned

Lukas von Hildebrandt. In the case of some of the Salzburg princes of the Church fame has a bitter taste, however. In 1731 Leopold Anton Eleutherius Baron of Firmian ordered the expulsion of all unbending Protestants: twenty thousand people had to leave the city and province of Salzburg; in their desperate search for a new home many found their death.

Finally, mention must be made of Hieronymus Colloredo who claims the doubtful honour of having made Mozart forever weary of Salzburg, his birthplace. During a visit to Vienna the archbishop called him a "scoundrel and a wretched youth" before showing him the door of the house of the Teutonic Order on 2nd May, 1781. In fact, a few years later Hieronymus Colloredo was to find out for himself how painful such an ejection can be: in 1800 he was forced to flee before Napoleon and three years later he relinquished his office in Vienna.

Thus came to an end the proud history of Salzburg as the principality of its archbishops. The city passed temporarily to Austria, then became Bavarian before in 1816 the Congress of Vienna fitted it into the red, white and red state pattern, more impressive in those days. But in Austria, too, the city on the Salzach has remained a cosmopolitan metropolis, relatively small, yet boundless. The princes of the Church have relinquished temporal power and the ruling lords have to share their authority today with directors, conductors and stage managers. Salzburg is still a world of its own, arousing a desire to experience it step by step, even if one shares this pleasure with many others. Anyone in the middle of the old town, in the Mozartplatz, listening to what the Glockenspiel and the fortress organ have to say to each other, also becomes a witness to the high-handedness of a prince bishop: during the demolition work Wolf Dietrich von Raichenau resided here in the "Neugebäude" (where today the somewhat less pompous Provincial Government is instal-

led), whilst the debris from the flattened houses of the citizenry piled up all around. Later, the square was named after the Michaelskirche and a good fifty years after Mozart's miserable death, when Salzburg – now Austrian – summoned a Munich sculptor, Ludwig Michael von Schwanthaler, to honour the city's great son with a memorial, the square acquired its present name. Only a few paces further on, the old city opens out with a sweeping gesture that is almost foreign into the Residenzplatz where the Residenzbrunnen, made of the finest Untersberger marble, stands almost forlorn in the large square, although it is one of the largest baroque fountains in the world. Since the cars have been shooed away into the Mönchsberg and only a couple of well-fed fiacre horses languorously clip their hooves here, the square has again recovered much of its original atmosphere: sublime presumption to the greater glory of God. Incidentally, even in overcrowded Salzburg it is no problem to evade the throng of the curious with a couple of smart steps. One such route leads through the courtyards of the Residenz – Haupthof, Toscanahof and Dietrichsruh – to the Wallistrakt and the stillness of St. Peter's.

It is really not the thing to by-pass the cathedral, however, so we come before its countenance and draw in our heads in admiration. Four powerful statues survey the bustle at their feet with stony composure: Peter and Paul pay honour to Rome near the main entrance, whilst Virgil and Rupert represent the bishopric of Salzburg. Above their heads the gable soars boldly upwards, flanked by two mighty towers, 82 metres high, crowned by cupolas. For fourteen years Santino Solari worked on this monumental building, erected on the foundations of the much larger Romanesque cathedral. Only the font came from the old building and it was over this bronze bowl that an infant called Wolfgang Amadeus received the sacrament. Upon entering, one feels at first a little lost in this costly spaciousness, sensing that here man is not the measure of all things. Beneath the huge, 64,5 metre dome this edifice seems to entirely evade earthly change, timeless and indestructible. In fact, however, Salzburg Cathedral lay in ruins twice in its long history; in 1944 hopefully for the last time, when an air raid caused the dome to collapse. Going out from the dim interior into the daylight, one is embraced by the festive unity of the Domplatz, for many years the grandiose yet intimate stage for the tale of the rich man's life and death.

The cathedral has an outwardly modest vis-à-vis: the Franciscan Church. Upon closer examination, however, it proves to be a many-faceted monument to various styles of building. In place of the Marienkirche, which was destroyed by fire, a massive Romanesque nave was erected in the 13th century, a richly arranged late Gothic chancel being added in the 15th century. Finally, in the 18th century, the interior was redecorated in opulent baroque. Fischer von Erlach designed the new altar, but could not bring himself to remove the beautiful Gothic madonna by the master, Michael Pacher. Removed from everything earthly, she thus thrones amidst the baroque splendour of this world, in her lap a child Jesus which was added at the end of the 19th century.

In the old princely city the Franziskanergasse and its continuation, the Hofstallgasse, form a majestic link between the Domplatz and the horse pond in the Siegmundsplatz. Running more or less parallel is its bourgeois, but by no means modest counterpart, the Getreidegasse. In the burghers' city the extravagant gesture is not so much in demand; dignified elegance and massive self-assurance define the scene more. The squares are small and comfortable, like the Waagplatz or the Alte Markt, a wondrously eccentric piece of the city with Salzburg's smallest house (no. 109) and the venerable court apothecary's, so mysteriously lovely that even purchasing aspirin there is an experience.

In Salzburg it only requires a few steps and a few minutes to pass from one world to the next. The Franziskanergasse is the transition from the Domplatz to the festival district and anyone turning off from it into the Wiener Philharmonikerstraße actually leaves it again: the lane used to be called the Marktgasse – it still smells like that – and it runs into the Universitätsplatz which, notwithstanding academic dignity, becomes a market square every morning. The Kollegienkirche, Fischer von Erlach's vast building with its central dome, gazes in blithe splendour at its profane opposite in playful rococo: Mozart's birthplace. Great changes were made to the front, at Getreidegasse no. 9, but the facade facing the Universitätsplatz was allowed to retain its old appearance. Once there, we can at once practise the art of walking through the Getreidegasse without becoming submerged in the all-engulfing stream of tourists. No passageway may be left out, one has to cross the street again and again, examining every inner courtyard. Apart from smart business acumen, a great deal of lovable individuality nestles in corners and passageways, beneath the vaulting. One has to raise one's head, too, to study the private wonderland of the arcades right up to the roof, the shape of houses that were allowed to grow before there was a dictate of straight lines and right angles. When the Getreidegasse joins the Bürgerspitalgasse, the Salzburg of ostentatious finery is abruptly over. No wonder: the old city ended after the Gstättentor, beyond that there were only fields and meadows. The tiny Badergäßchen, incidentally, provides a reminder of truly far-sighted municipal hygiene: the inmates of the nearby Bürgerspital were allowed to take a steam bath in the poor people's bath there – three times a year, what is more.

Whereas the high clergy kept to themselves in the old city, the burghers' town soon claimed the other bank of the Salzach. Even in Roman days there was a footbridge

across the river and a wooden bridge has been documented since 1090. The "new town" is thus pretty old – after all, the little Platzl, source of the Linzer Gasse and the narrow, winding Steingasse, was a creation of Wolf Dietrich's. He had houses pulled down in this area, too, in order to make room for a respectable bridgehead. The new town did not lack famous inhabitants either: Platzl no. 3 was the address of the famous physician, researcher and philosopher, Theophrastus Paracelsus von Hohenheim, who finally came to rest in the Sebastianskirche in the Linzer Gasse. Its cemetery harbours the graves of Leopold Mozart, the composer's father, and Konstanze, Mozart's wife. Here, too, is the Sebastianskapelle which Wolf Dietrich had erected as his tomb, an outwardly simple building with a costly interior. But the archbishop also gave a thought to a dwelling of a more sensual nature: Salome Alt, Wolf Dietrich's mistress and later his wife, lived with her fifteen children in Schloß Altenau which was built for her. When Markus Sittikus succeeded to the imprisoned Wolf Dietrich, he turned the hussy out of the palace and gave it a new name: Mirabell.

Steingasse no. 9 was the birthplace of Josef Mohr, composer of the Christmas carol "Stille Nacht, heilige Nacht" and the house where Mozart lived can be found in the Makartplatz which is dominated by Fischer von Erlach's Dreifaltigkeitskirche. Only the so-called "Tanzmeistersaal" has remained intact. Mozart is also present here in a somewhat curious fashion: the Viennese summerhouse belonging to his librettist Schikaneder was given to the city of Salzburg in 1873, Mozart having worked in it when composing the Magic Flute. It first stood on the Kapuzinerberg and today it can be found hidden behind the Mirabell Gardens in the Schwarzstraße. But let us enter that green, colourful paradise: the side of the palace facing the gardens has retained its Lukas von Hildebrandt facade which blends in bright, well ordered harmony with the architecture of the park. Here the Pegasus fountain can be found, once part of the horse pond in the Kapitelplatz; here, too, the 18th century topiary can be admired, some of the oldest of its kind. This leads us to the scurrilous garden of dwarfs. Decimated by rude collecting passion, its throng of ill-humoured and mis-shapen gnomes give an oppressive view of what their Lordships once found amusing.

Between the beautiful, venerable, marvellous Salzburg and the banal, hardly interesting, frequently rather ugly Salzburg which also exists there lurks another, quietly unobtrusive reality: areas in which the city lives inwardly, silently, wisely and not without comfort. The Kapuziner-berg comes to mind with its simple monastery and its almost alpine ridge upon which even a family of chamois feel at home and where a fortified site from the Thirty Years War, the Franciscischlößl, retains its dignified appearance, even as a snack bar. Nonnberg convent, the oldest community of nuns north of the Alps, is one of Salzburg's interior worlds with tranquil depths. The doorkeeper opens the church to strangers, but the nuns live in strict seclusion.

On the Mönchsberg everyone can do as he wishes, but the tourists stay in Café Winkler or in the casino because the world round about only has bucolic peace to offer, nothing spectacular, apart from the magnificent view over the rooftops of the city. In order to enjoy this, however, one has to walk a few steps and that, again, is going too far for most people. At any rate, why should one observe the city from above, when one can take part in the histrionics down below as an actor in this gripping and engrossing production? Salzburg and the people of Salzburg are masters in the art of entertaining and occupying curious guests with showpieces and spectacles of all kinds in order, untouched by all this, to preserve their own private life.

Sincere friends of this city, those who neither push in nor intrude, may nevertheless hope to be asked in one day.

Alfred Komarek

VIEWS OF THE CITY

View of the Cathedral and the Fortress from the Imbergstiege leading up to the Kapuzinerberg

17

View from the Mönchsberg across the Salzach and Elisabethkai to the Kapuzinerberg

The old city with the Kollegienkirche, the Glockenspiel tower, the Cathedral and the Franciscan Church

The Franciscan Church, Kollegienkirche, Cathedral and Nonnberg Collegiate Church disappearing in the mist

20

The dome of St. Peter's in front of the fortress

Rudolfskai, towered over by the Cathedral, fortress, Glockenspiel tower and Nonnberg Church

Evening on the Salzach

The new University of Salzburg, Faculty of Science

THE WORK OF ART PLEASING TO GOD

Gothic triptych in Nonnberg Collegiate Church (originally in the affiliated church of Scheffau)

Above: the Maximus Chapel in
the catacombs of St. Peter's
Below: St. Peter's "Stiftskeller",
probably Salzburg's oldest inn

St. Peter's cemetery

Gothic chancel of the Franciscan Church

30

Above: Madonna (Michael Pacher, 1496, child Jesus figure added in 1895) from the high altar of the Franciscan Church
Below: Foot of the pulpit (c. 1220) in the Franciscan Church

Inside the Cathedral

Salzburg Cathedral was built between 1614 and 1655 according to Santino Solari's plans. Its facade was much copied

The festival season

The Residenzbrunnen (1656–1661), one of Austria's loveliest fountains; its creator is unknown

Erected in 1696–1707, the Kollegienkirche (right) is J. B. Fischer von Erlach's main work in Salzburg

Detail on the altar of Mülln Parish Church

The Gothic tower (with baroque dome) of Mülln Parish Church

Tower and dome of St. Peter's Collegiate Church

WHERE OLD WALLS BREATHE

The traditional Café Glockenspiel in the Mozartplatz

41

In the Alter Markt

In the Residenzplatz

Three times a day (at 7, 11 and 6) tunes are played on the 35 bells of the Glockenspiel

Gstättengasse

Getreidegasse

Entertainer in the Residenzplatz

In the castle courtyard of Hohensalzburg

Audience room in the Residenz

SALZBURG, CITY OF THE MUSES

Mozart composing the Requiem, painting by James Grant, 1854; Salzburg Museum Carolino Augusteum

Horse pond and former court stables, now part of the Festival Hall

The Mozart monument in the Mozartplatz, cast by J. Stiglmaier in 1842 after a model by L. Schwanthaler

The Judengasse in the festival season

"Jedermann"

"Jedermann" performance in front of the Cathedral

Salzburg, festively illuminated

In Mozart's birthplace

Advent carols by the "Salzburger Hirtenbuam" in the large Festival Hall

CASTLES OF ENCHANTMENT

In the entrance hall of Schloß Mirabell

a)/b) The Mirabell Gardens, designed by Fischer von Erlach in 1690; c) Garden of dwarfs near Schloß Mirabell;
d) Copies of the Borghesian fencers by Michael Bernhard and Andreas Götzinger in the Mirabell Gardens

Staircase with figures by Georg Raphael Donner in Schloß Mirabell

Schloß Hellbrunn, octagonal pavilion, frescos by Donato Arsenio Mascagni

Water amusements in the gardens of Hellbrunn, built by Archbishop Markus Sittikus in 1613–1615

Reception room in Schloß Leopoldskron

The late baroque site of Leopoldskron with the fortress of Hohensalzburg in the background

Schloß Kleßheim, built by J. B. Fischer von Erlach in 1700–1709

INCIDENTAL IDYLLS

Hellbrunn Avenue

On the Kapuzinerberg

View of the Hochstaufen from the Gaisberg

Hoarfrost on the Heuberg

View of Hohensalzburg fortress from the Gaisberg

On the Mönchsberg

Farmhouse on the Gaisberg

The "Krauthäusl", former common keeper's cottage belonging to St. Peter's Abbey

Front cover photograph:
Pegasus (Kaspar Gras, 1661) in the Mirabell Gardens

English translation: Jacqueline Schweighofer.

© Copyright 1995 by Pinguin-Verlag
A-6021 Innsbruck
All rights reserved
Printing and binding: Druckerei Theiss, A-9400 Wolfsberg
Colour reproductions: Tiroler Repro, A-6020 Innsbruck
Typesetting: Lasersatz Maringer, A-5751 Maishofen
Printed in Austria
ISBN 3-7016-2442-9